# Timeline of key events

The Viking age lasted from the 8th century to the 11th century.

Cross-shaped pendant

## Vikings settle permanently in England
The Vikings started their own kingdom in Britain with Jorvik (York) as their capital.

## Greenlanders and Icelanders convert to Christianity
Some people still worshipped the old gods alongside the Christian god.

## Harald Hardrada is killed
Harald was killed by Harold II of England, who was then killed by William the Conqueror. William became king of England.

William the Conqueror

| 876CE | 930CE | 981CE | 1000 | 1001 | 1047 | 1066 |

## The first *Thing* assembly takes place in Iceland
The present-day Icelandic parliament is called the Althing.

## Explorer Leif the Lucky lands in Newfoundland
Leif was the first European to visit North America.

## Harald Hardrada becomes King of Norway
Harald was a bold warrior. In 1047 he defeated his enemies to become the king of Norway.

A statue of Erik the Red

## Erik the Red explores Greenland and sets up a colony
After being cast out of Iceland, Erik sailed west to find a new place to settle.

Harald Hardrada fighting King Harold at the Battle of Stamford Bridge, England.

Things to find out:

# DK findout!
# Vikings

Author: Philip Steele

Consultant: Dr Ragnhild Ljosland

**Project editors** Satu Hämeenaho-Fox, Roohi Sehgal
**Editor** Radhika Haswani
**Project art editors** Emma Hobson, Radhika Banerjee
**Art editor** Mohd Zishan
**DTP designers** Dheeraj Singh,
Mohd Rizwan, Vijay Kandwal
**Picture researcher** Sumita Khatwani
**Jacket co-ordinator** Francesca Young
**Jacket designer** Suzena Sengupta
**Educational consultant** Jacqueline Harris
**Managing editors** Laura Gilbert, Monica Saigal
**Managing art editor** Diane Peyton Jones
**Deputy managing art editor** Ivy Sengupta
**Senior Pre-production Producer** Luca Frassinetti
**Senior producer** Isabell Schart
**Creative director** Helen Senior
**Publishing director** Sarah Larter

First published in Great Britain in 2018 by
Dorling Kindersley Limited
80 Strand, London, WC2R 0RL

Copyright © 2018 Dorling Kindersley Limited
A Penguin Random House Company
18 19 10 9 8 7 6 5 4 3 2 1
001–308822–Sept/2018

A CIP catalogue record for this book
is available from the British Library.
ISBN: 978-0-2413-2302-1

Printed and bound in China

A WORLD OF IDEAS:
SEE ALL THERE IS TO KNOW

www.dk.com

# Contents

**Thor's hammer charm**

Drinking horn

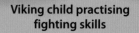

**Viking child practising fighting skills**

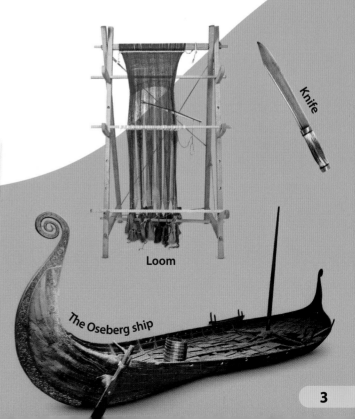

Knife

Loom

The Oseberg ship

**Stave church in Norway**

# Who were the Vikings?

In the Middle Ages, the people of Europe's far north were farmers and sailors. From the 790s they began to attack neighbouring lands, killing people and stealing their treasure. The Vikings are remembered as fierce warriors, but they made history in other ways too, as traders, explorers, craft workers, and storytellers.

## How did the Vikings get their name?

Viking meant "raiding" or "raider". They were also known as "Northmen". Today we use the word Viking to describe Scandinavian people in the time between about 790 and 1050.

**The Vikings attacking Paris**

**Warriors**
Viking fighters were mostly part-time warriors who left their farms to go raiding.

**Children**
Kids didn't go to school, but had to learn skills such as farming or weaving.

**Traders**
Viking merchants traded far from home, including in Greenland, Russia, and Baghdad.

**Farmers**
The Vikings were skilled farmers, even in lands with harsh weather.

**Settlers**
You needed to be tough and brave to leave home and move to an unknown land.

## Viking community
Many Vikings lived in remote farms, linked only by muddy tracks or waterways. Where the farmland was good, there were more people, and trading towns grew up around ports.

**Rulers**
Power was held by leaders called jarls, local assemblies called Things, and by chiefs and kings.

**Parents and babies**
Strong family bonds helped Vikings survive cold winters in Scandinavia and Greenland.

### FACT FILE

» **Who:** The Vikings

» **When:** The Middle Ages, between about 790 and 1050

» **Where:** Originally in Denmark, Sweden, and Norway

» **What:** Raided overseas, in Great Britain, Ireland, France, Iceland, and Greenland

» **Language:** Old Norse

**Greenland**
In about 982, Erik the Red explored this bleak and icy land. He named it Greenland to persuade other Vikings to move there. The first permanent settlement was made in 985.

**Iceland**
Viking seafarers, fishermen, and farmers made their homes in Iceland between about 870 and 930.

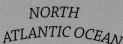

*NORTH ATLANTIC OCEAN*

**Canada**
Erik's son Leif the Lucky sailed to what is now Canada. He probably explored Baffin Bay, Labrador, and Newfoundland in 1001.

**Ireland**
Vikings raided Ireland from the 790s, and by 845 had founded a town at Dublin. They also settled around Wexford, Waterford, Cork, and Limerick.

■ **Viking homelands**

# Viking voyages

The Viking homelands were surrounded by seas and had deep, narrow inland waters called fjords. This meant the Vikings had to learn to be sailors and shipbuilders. Their warriors and traders sailed long distances to discover new lands. In some places they built settlements, which were places for Viking people to live.

**! WOW!**

It took about **seven days** to sail from Scandinavia to **Iceland**.

**The Faroe Islands**
The remote Faroe islands were settled by Viking sheep farmers in about 800.

**Scotland and the Isle of Man**
Vikings from Norway took over Scotland's far north, the Shetland and Orkney Islands, and the Isle of Man.

ARCTIC OCEAN

**Norway**
Norwegian Vikings lived by the fjords of the west coast.

**Sweden**
Swedish Vikings farmed in the southeast and on islands in the Baltic Sea.

BALTIC SEA

**England**
By 876, a large area of England, known as the Danelaw, was under Viking rule.

**Russia**
Vikings from Sweden, known as Varangians, traded with the Slavs of Russia and eastern Europe.

**Denmark**
Danish Vikings lived in the far south of the Viking homelands.

**Constantinople**
This city (modern Istanbul) was capital of the Byzantine Empire. The Vikings called it Miklagard, the Great City.

**Wales**
Wales was raided by the Vikings from 850.

**France**
Viking armies put Paris under siege in 845 and 885–886. In 910 they were given a large area of France called Normandy.

**Southern Europe**
Viking raiders and traders sailed into the Mediterranean Sea.

# Medieval neighbours

The Vikings lived alongside many other medieval powers. In the 800s, the Frankish emperor Charlemagne ruled a huge area of France, Germany, and Italy. Most of Spain was ruled by Muslims called the Moors. In the 800s, the Anglo-Saxon King Alfred of Wessex fought against large armies of Viking invaders in Britain.

Charlemagne

King Alfred

# Longship

The longship was a narrow boat designed for speed. The underside was flat enough to sail up a river without hitting the riverbed, and could be dragged up onto a beach. The longship was ideal for raiding, but a wider, sturdier ship called a knarr was used for carrying cargo.

**! WOW!**

A longship could move at up to **28 km/h (17 miles an hour).**

**6**

**3**

**1**

**5**

**4**

**2**

**Overlapping planks**
Each plank, or strake, overlapped the next, and was secured by nails and rivets.

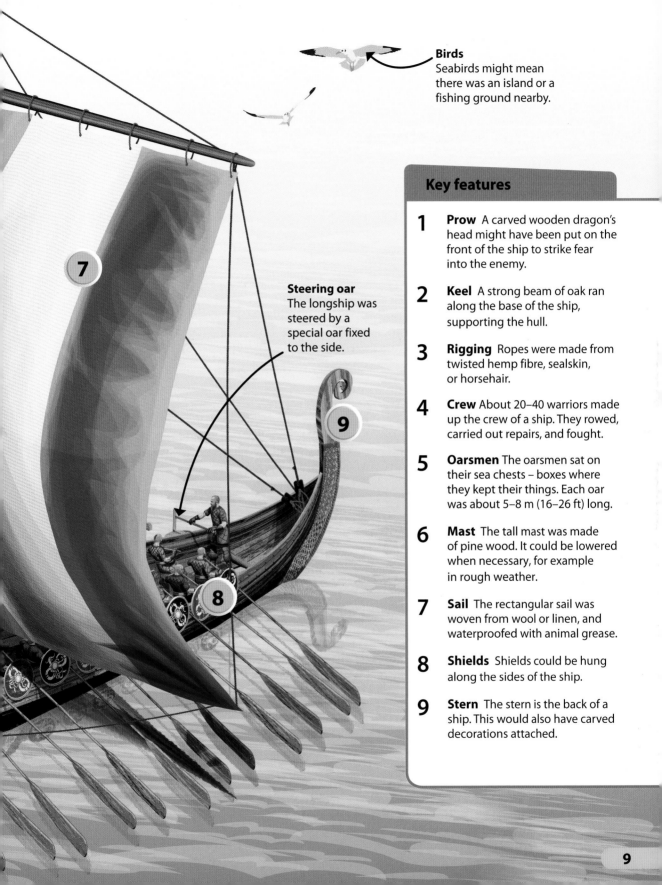

**Birds**
Seabirds might mean there was an island or a fishing ground nearby.

**Steering oar**
The longship was steered by a special oar fixed to the side.

## Key features

**1** **Prow** A carved wooden dragon's head might have been put on the front of the ship to strike fear into the enemy.

**2** **Keel** A strong beam of oak ran along the base of the ship, supporting the hull.

**3** **Rigging** Ropes were made from twisted hemp fibre, sealskin, or horsehair.

**4** **Crew** About 20–40 warriors made up the crew of a ship. They rowed, carried out repairs, and fought.

**5** **Oarsmen** The oarsmen sat on their sea chests – boxes where they kept their things. Each oar was about 5–8 m (16–26 ft) long.

**6** **Mast** The tall mast was made of pine wood. It could be lowered when necessary, for example in rough weather.

**7** **Sail** The rectangular sail was woven from wool or linen, and waterproofed with animal grease.

**8** **Shields** Shields could be hung along the sides of the ship.

**9** **Stern** The stern is the back of a ship. This would also have carved decorations attached.

# Raids

Around 1,200 years ago, the sight of longships caused panic along the coasts of Britain and Ireland. In a raid, Viking warriors quickly landed and stormed ashore with swords and axes in their hands. The villagers had no time to escape. The Vikings murdered people, or kidnapped them to be slaves, looted (stole) valuable objects, and set buildings on fire.

## 3 STAGES OF RAIDING

**1**  **790s** Small groups of Vikings leave their homelands in the summer months to raid islands, coastal villages, and monasteries in Britain.

**2**  **840s** Larger bands of Vikings build camps overseas. They can now raid and trade all year round. They have a base at Dublin, Ireland, from 841.

**3**  **840s–880s** Raiders join together to form armies. They even attack big cities, including Paris and London.

## Surprise attack

On 8 June 793, Vikings from Norway launched an attack on Lindisfarne, an island off the coast of England. The raiders burnt the Christian monastery there. This carving shows the raid.

# Ill-gotten gains

Viking raiders made their fortunes by stealing valuable gold and silver, as well as food and cattle. Longships were designed for a quick getaway after a raid.

**Viking treasure chest**

This small casket once held the holy relics of a Christian saint. A relic was a body part of a saint or something that belonged to them. The casket was seized in Ireland or Scotland, and carried back to Denmark. Other precious items stolen from churches included crosses, silver dishes, and bells.

**A hugely valuable hoard of gold jewellery**

Norway's biggest Viking treasure hoard was buried in the 860s and found in 1834. A hoard is a collection of treasure. Gold and silver were valuable and easy to melt down to make into new things. Whoever owned this hoard buried it but never came back for it.

# Warriors and weapons

Most Viking men were not full-time fighters, but they all knew how to use a weapon when needed. They could be called up for a raiding voyage as early as the age od 15. Vikings mostly fought on foot, using swords, axes, or spears.

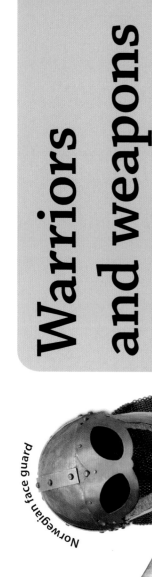

Norwegian face guard

## Helmet
Iron helmets could be round or cone-shaped. Some had a bar to protect the nose, or a full faceguard.

## Axe
Battle-axes had long or short hafts (wooden handles), and iron heads with sharp blades.

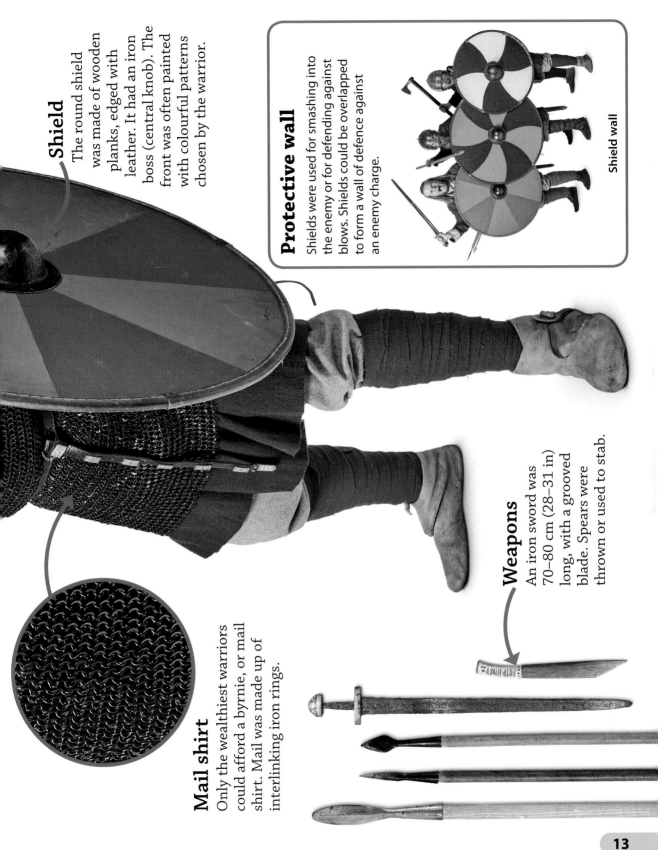

## Shield

The round shield was made of wooden planks, edged with leather. It had an iron boss (central knob). The front was often painted with colourful patterns chosen by the warrior.

## Protective wall

Shields were used for smashing into the enemy or for defending against blows. Shields could be overlapped to form a wall of defence against an enemy charge.

Shield wall

## Mail shirt

Only the wealthiest warriors could afford a byrnie, or mail shirt. Mail was made up of interlinking iron rings.

## Weapons

An iron sword was 70–80 cm (28–31 in) long, with a grooved blade. Spears were thrown or used to stab.

# Traders

Vikings travelled across Europe and beyond to buy and sell goods. They sailed along the coasts and down rivers. Merchants sold goods to other Vikings in their homelands in Scandinavia, and some traders went as far away as Russia and Arabia.

**Greenland**
In Greenland, the Vikings braved ice and freezing temperatures to hunt walruses. Walrus tusks were very valuable. They could be carved into delicate figures, such as this chesspiece.

Walrus ivory chesspiece

**England**
The Vikings bought wool from the British for their weaving, as well as using wool from their own sheep. Wool was needed to make all sorts of important things, from warm winter cloaks to sails for ships.

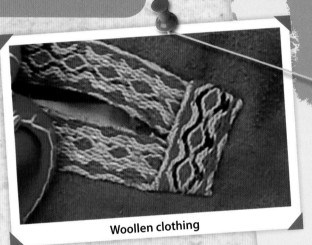

Woollen clothing

 **WOW!**

If Vikings found rivers were blocked, they **carried their ships** over the land instead.

**Germany**
Drinking glasses for the rich were brought back to Scandinavia from the Rhineland area of Germany, along with barrels of wine to drink. Craft workers also used glass to make beads.

Glass

**Eastern Europe**
In the Viking age, honey was widely traded. It was the only way to sweeten food and was used to make mead, a favourite drink of the Vikings.

Honey

**Russia**
Fur from animals that lived in Russian forests, such as wolves, was worth a lot of money. The fur was made into warm clothes for the winter months.

Silver coins

**Damascus and Baghdad**
The Viking homelands had no silver mines. Much of the silver they used was recycled from coins originally traded in the Middle East.

**Arabia**
Long-distance trade brought rare spices and fine silks to northern Europe from the Middle East and Constantinople. Silk and spices were very expensive, so only rich people could afford them.

Silk and spices

# Myth busters

Ideas about how the Vikings looked and behaved are not always right. A lot of myths have been invented by modern films and computer games. These myths usually have very little to do with the everyday lives of real Vikings.

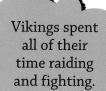

Vikings spent all of their time raiding and fighting.

Vikings loved feasting and fighting, and were not very skilled in art and making things.

Viking warriors went into battle wearing helmets with horns, to make themselves look fierce.

Viking warriors were a scruffy lot, with shaggy hair, tangled beards, and ragged clothes.

The Vikings were the most bloodthirsty and aggressive people in medieval Europe.

This was a man's world. Viking women had no rights.

The Vikings were probably no worse than other medieval people. Christian writers may have thought the first raiders were evil because they worshipped many gods. The Vikings later became Christians.

Figurine of the god Freyr

They may have looked a bit scruffy after a long sea voyage, but generally Viking men and women were clean, groomed, and well-dressed.

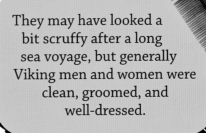
Viking comb

Most Vikings spent their lives working hard on the farm, fishing, trading, and raising children.

Silver coin for trading

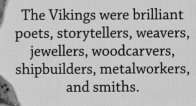
Gold necklace

The Vikings were brilliant poets, storytellers, weavers, jewellers, woodcarvers, shipbuilders, metalworkers, and smiths.

Men held power, but women had rights within marriage and were respected. They ran the household when the men were away fighting, and travelled to new lands to create settlements.

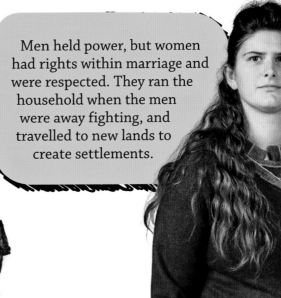
Viking woman

Warriors in history did sometimes wear horned helmets – but not the Vikings. The horns were an invention of 19th-century artists.

Helmet with face guard

# Famous Vikings

Some Vikings were more brave, wise, or just more dangerous than the rest. These famous Vikings were talked about in ancient tales called sagas. Vikings who attacked other countries were talked about in history books written by those who survived.

## RAGNAR LOTHBROK

**Who was he?** King, raider
**Fame:** No one knows if Ragnar was real or a legend. He was known for attacking Franks and Saxons. The tales say that Ragnar was killed by being thrown into a snake pit by King Aella of Northumbria. If he was real, he died in about 865.
**Facts:** Lothbrok means "hairy breeches"!

## ROLLO

**Who was he?** First Duke of Normandy
**Fame:** Rollo (c.870–930) was the leader of the Danish Vikings who settled in France. He was given the title of Duke of Normandy to stop him from attacking the Franks. His people went on to be called the Normans.
**Fact:** Rollo was too big to ride on a horse, so he walked everywhere.

## UNN KETILSDOTTIR

**Who was she?** Clever pioneer
**Fame:** After her family were attacked and killed, Unn had a ship built in secret and sailed it to Iceland to create a new Viking settlement.
**Fact:** She was known as "Unn the Deep-Minded" because she was wise.

## ERIK THE RED

**Who was he?** Outlaw, seafarer, pioneer
**Fame:** Erik Thorvaldsson (950–1003) was nicknamed "Erik the Red" because of his red beard. He was the first person to sail to Greenland and start settlements there.
**Fact:** His son was the explorer Leif the Lucky.

## ÅSA HARALDSDOTTIR

**Who was she?** Queen of Agder, Norway
**Fame:** Princesss Åsa was kidnapped by Gudrød of Borre to be his wife. But she had him murdered and went back to her home of Agder to rule for 20 years. She may have died in about 834.
**Fact:** It's possible that Åsa is the woman buried in the Oseberg ship burial.

## HARALD HARDRADA

**Who was he?** King of Norway
**Fame:** Harald (born in 1015) spent years in exile from Norway. He fought in Russia and in the Byzantine Empire, where he had many adventures. Harald became King of Norway in 1046 and was killed while trying to invade England in 1066.
**Fact:** Hardrada means "stern ruler".

## Scary nicknames

The Vikings got nicknames based on the way they looked or behaved. Ragnar Lothbrok's son Björn Ironside was known for being a warrior, so his nickname described his armour. The violent Erik Bloodaxe murdered his seven brothers. Sigrid the Ambitious wanted to be a powerful queen. Can you think up some nicknames for you and your friends?

# Walls and forts

The Vikings built long walls to defend Denmark from invaders, and dug ditches around their settlements. At least seven ring forts have been discovered in Denmark, Norway, and southern Sweden. They date from about 958 to 986, when Harald Bluetooth ruled these lands. The forts may have been built to control his people as well as protect them from others.

## Fort from the past

Sweden's Trelleborgen ring fort was discovered in 1988. When archaeologists had finished examining the fort, experts decided to rebuild a section of the walls using only basic tools. The fort was built on a mound 6 m (20 ft) high and covered with timbers.

The rebuilt
Trelleborgen gatehouse

## FORT FEATURES

**1** **Ditch** This was 4 m (13 ft) deep and 17 m (56 ft) wide. It was not filled with water, but did have a wooden fence for protection.

**2** **Ramparts** These protective walls were circular and measured 137 m (449 ft) from side to side. They were 5 m (16 ft) high and covered with wooden logs.

**3** **Gates** Each ring fort had a north, south, east, and west gate. They were designed with narrow bridges to make them easy to defend against attackers.

**4** **Roads** The ring was cut into quarters by two straight roads paved with wood. Another road may have run around the edge.

**5** **Buildings** These included houses, workshops, and stables. Some of the buildings housed warriors.

**6** **River** Low, marshy ground lay on either side of the fort, which made it difficult to approach.

**7** **Surroundings** The original fort had 15 buildings outside its walls, and a cemetery.

# Viking society

Early Viking kings ruled fairly small regions. For many years there was no powerful central government. For most communities, it was the local chieftain, or jarl, who was in charge. Free citizens were called karls. Slaves were called thralls.

## Royal power

In the 900s and 1000s, the Viking homelands were ruled by powerful Christian kings. King Knut the Great (c.995–1035) ruled Denmark, Norway, and England. Under the king were three tiers of society.

**Karls**
The karls were the largest social class. They were ordinary people and could be rich or poor. They worked as farmers, merchants, shipbuilders, smiths, or woodcarvers. They also joined longship crews and went raiding.

**Thralls**
Thralls were slaves bought by traders or captured in raids. It was possible for someone to move up or down through Viking society. Some thralls were karls who had got into debt. Sometimes a thrall could save up money to buy his or her freedom.

**Jarls**
Jarls were the wealthiest class of people. They owned large areas of land and many ships. They wore fine clothes and had the best armour. They could call up karls to join raiding bands or armies.

# The law of the land

A public gathering called a Thing was held in each region. It had a leader called the Lawspeaker and only men who were jarls or karls could attend. The Thing passed new laws and judged crimes. For example, it made thieves pay back money they had stolen. It ordered criminals to leave the country as exiles, or made them outlaws with no rights. Arguments could be settled by armed combat.

**! WOW!**

Iceland has the **world's oldest parliament,** the **Althingi.** It began as a Viking assembly in 930.

# At home

Viking towns were home to up to 2,000 people, but most Vikings lived in the countryside. Farmers built bigger homes than town-dwellers. These homes, called longhouses, were shared by children, parents, grandparents, farm workers, and often animals.

**Pottery lamp**

**Oil lamp**
Inside the longhouse, it was dark and smoky, but there was flickering light from pottery lamps, brought to the Viking lands by traders.

## The longhouse
A longhouse was built from local materials, often with timber beams. The walls were made of planks, or wattle-and-daub (sticks plastered with mud).

**Loom**
Women of all ages spun wool and wove textiles to make clothes, blankets, and wall hangings.

**Hearth**
A firepit was the centre of the home. It was used for cooking, heating, and light. Smoke escaped through a hole in the roof.

Iron pots were used for cooking.

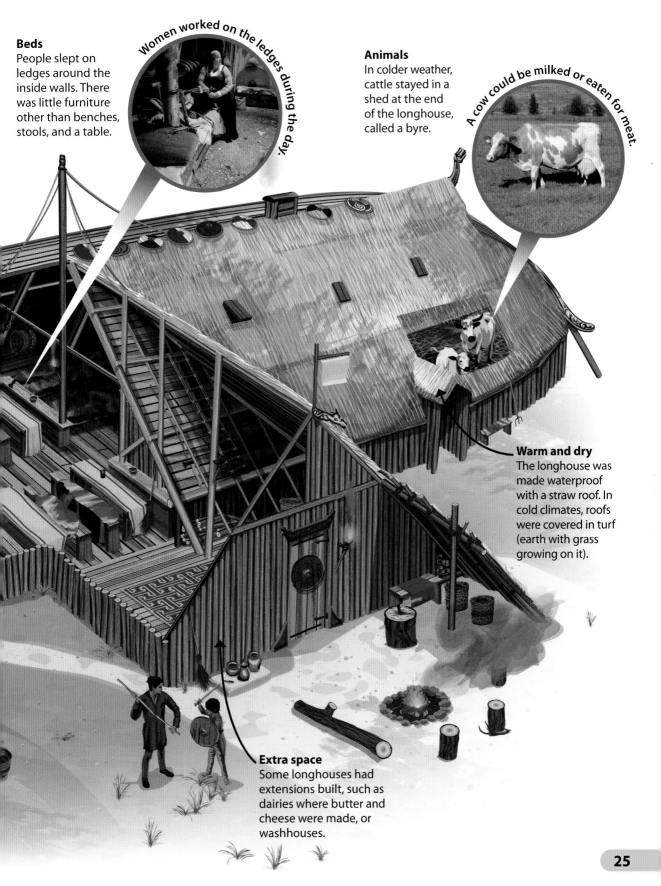

**Beds**
People slept on ledges around the inside walls. There was little furniture other than benches, stools, and a table.

Women worked on the ledges during the day.

**Animals**
In colder weather, cattle stayed in a shed at the end of the longhouse, called a byre.

A cow could be milked or eaten for meat.

**Warm and dry**
The longhouse was made waterproof with a straw roof. In cold climates, roofs were covered in turf (earth with grass growing on it).

**Extra space**
Some longhouses had extensions built, such as dairies where butter and cheese were made, or washhouses.

# Jobs and skills

Viking men and women were amazingly skilled in all kinds of craft work. They knew how to handle the tools of their trade, whether these were chisels for carving, anvils for hammering metal, or looms for weaving cloth. Viking designs were very artistic and often inspired by animals. They were hard workers too, using only muscle power as there were no electric tools.

## Boat building

It took many men to build a longship. First, they cut down the best trees in the forest. Then they hauled the logs to the water's edge. Using axes and chisels, they cut the logs into wedge-shaped planks. They carved a prow to go at the front of the ship.

## Blacksmith

The blacksmith was one of the most important workers in any Viking settlement. He heated iron until it was soft, hammered it into shape on an anvil, and then let it cool and harden. He made knives, axes, nails, pots, and pans. Good quality iron could be bought from mines in Sweden. Impure "bog iron" was found in many local wetlands.

Hammers, files, and tongs

# WEAVING

Women wove tunics, cloaks and wall-hangings. These were made on an upright wooden frame called a loom. The woollen warp had up and down threads. The weft threads were woven in between the warp threads, and pushed upwards to make the cloth.

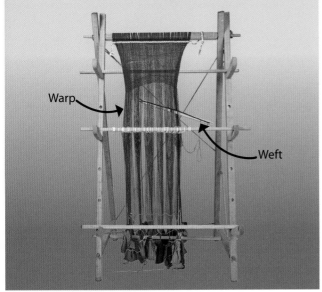

Warp

Weft

# Farming

Viking farmers and thralls (slaves) worked hard on the land. They grew barley, rye, and oats. They planted seeds in the spring and harvested crops in the autumn. Viking sheep shed their wool in the summer and this was collected to be used for weaving.

Scythe

# Dyeing

The Vikings liked to wear bright colours. They used wild flowers, lichen, roots, and leaves to make dyes. Yellow dye came from the plant weld, blue from a plant called woad, and red from the root of the madder plant.

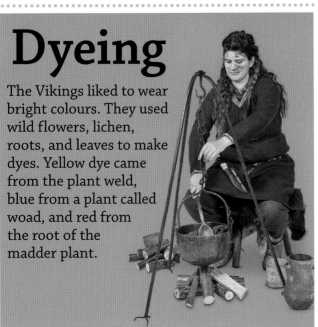

# MAKING JEWELLERY

Jewellers worked in silver and gold, or in pewter – a cheaper mixture of tin and lead. They could decorate one metal with another, create swirling patterns, and polish metal to be shiny. They used amber, jet, gemstones, or coloured glass.

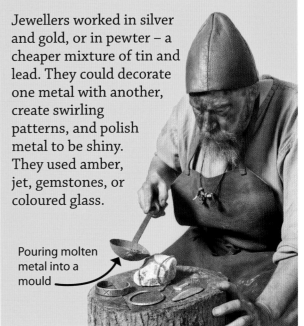

Pouring molten metal into a mould

# Viking feast

A high-born jarl loved to feast on mutton (sheep), pork, beef, or goat meat. Most ordinary people lived off porridge, rough bread, cheese, fish, and vegetables. They ate from wooden bowls and plates.

## Fruit
People collected wild berries, such as bilberries and strawberries, from the forests.

## Eggs
Farmers raised chickens, ducks, and geese. Wild birds' eggs were eaten too. The nests of seabirds were raided from cliff ledges.

## Vegetables
Leeks, peas, onions, and beans were grown, but were probably a bit tougher than the ones we eat today. Many wild plants and herbs were also gathered.

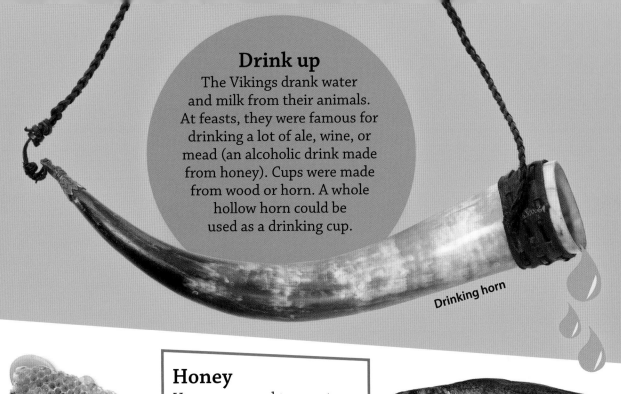

## Drink up

The Vikings drank water and milk from their animals. At feasts, they were famous for drinking a lot of ale, wine, or mead (an alcoholic drink made from honey). Cups were made from wood or horn. A whole hollow horn could be used as a drinking cup.

Drinking horn

## Honey

Honey was used to sweeten food and drinks. Sugar made from cane was not known in Europe until the 1400s.

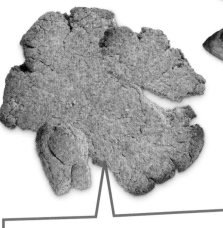

## Fish

Fish were caught with a line or in nets. The seas and lakes were full of fish such as herring. They could be saved for later by drying, smoking, or salting.

## Bread

Flour was ground from barley, oats, rye, and wheat. Sometimes seeds were added. The bread was baked on a hot stone.

# Viking animals

Both wild and tame animals played a big part in the lives of the Vikings. Farmers raised sheep, goats, pigs, and cattle for meat and milk. The Vikings hunted hares, wild birds, elk, and reindeer. They fished the rich northern seas and hunted walrus in Greenland.

## Brown bear
These fierce giants were hunted in northern forests for their fur.

## Manx Loaghtan sheep
Viking settlers made most of their clothes from wool, and bred tough sheep like this one.

## Norwegian Elkhound
These dogs were used for hunting elk and other large animals, guarding property, and herding on the farm.

## Gyrfalcon

The Vikings were great falconers, using birds of prey to hunt other birds and small animals. The gyrfalcon came from Greenland and other Arctic lands.

## Wild boar

Beware the charge of this wild pig! Early Vikings hunted boars for their meat.

## Norwegian Forest cat

Cats were used to catch mice on farms. Scandinavian cats developed long hair to stay warm in the snow.

# Wondrous beasts

Viking myths are full of magical animals, and pictures of them were often carved in wood and stone. The chariot of the goddess Freyja was pulled by two cats. She had a boar called Hildisvíni and wore a cloak of falcon feathers.

**Wise ravens**
Hugin and Munin were ravens that flew around the world as the spies of Odin, the king of the gods.

**Odin's super-steed**
Sleipnir was the fastest of all horses, with eight strong legs.

**Serpent of the world**
In Viking myth, a huge snake wrapped itself around the whole world, with its tail in its mouth.

**Dragons**
Snarling dragons were popular in Viking art. Dragon heads were carved on the prows of longships, to strike fear into the enemy.

# Viking women

Women did not have equal power in Viking society and could not attend the Thing. But free women, who were not slaves, had rights and were highly respected. They ran the house and farm, and were tough pioneers in new settlements.

## Hair and cap

Hair was washed and combed. Married free women tied back their long hair and wore a cap, a scarf, or a hood.

A gold brooch

## Brooches

Beautiful brooches were used to fasten the shoulder straps to the front of the tunic. They also showed off the wearer's wealth.

## Household accounts

Women were in charge of the money. They could own property, and divorce their husbands if they wanted to.

Money pouch

Ornate key

## Key chain

Keys, often hung from the belt, were symbols of a woman's authority in the home. Many keys were beautifully made.

## Clothing

Women wore a long shift made of wool or linen, and a shorter woollen over-tunic with shoulder straps.

## In the home

Women ruled the home. They prepared food, cooked, cleaned, and did the spinning and weaving to make clothes. They also looked after the children.

## On the farm

Men did most of the farming, but women helped with many tasks on the farm, such as milking and collecting eggs.

## Lucky charms

From an early age, Vikings wore charms around their necks to ward off illness, injury, or bad luck. When the Vikings became Christians, they wore both crosses and symbols such as Thor's hammer.

**Thor's hammer**
Thor used his hammer to defeat the giants. Little hammer pendants were worn for good luck.

# Growing up

Little Viking children played with toys, woollen balls, wooden animals, or dolls. As they grew up they could swim in the lake or play boardgames. They didn't go to school, but had to work hard on the farm.

**Naming ceremony**
Babies were welcomed into the family and Viking society at a special naming ceremony.

The baby was given a name on around the ninth night after birth.

The father of a new-born baby would wrap it in his cloak to show he would care for it.

Water was sprinkled on the new baby. The baby might also be given gifts.

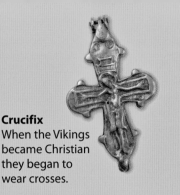

**Crucifix**
When the Vikings became Christian they began to wear crosses.

**Valkyrie**
This charm shows a Valkyrie, a woman who takes dead warriors to Odin's hall in Asgard.

Swords and spears were made of blunt wood, to avoid injuries.

Children practised with older relatives as well as others their own age.

## Warrior in training
Boys were taught to fight at an early age, wrestling, leaping, and ducking. By the age of 15, they were fit for battle.

Defence was as important as attack. Clever tactics could save lives and win battles.

Strength was built up by regular training sessions.

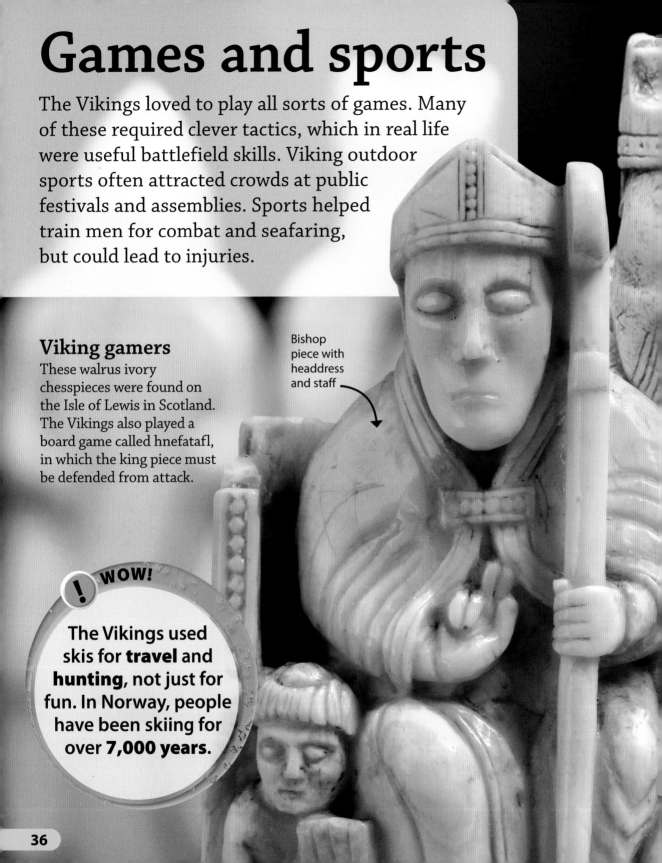

# Games and sports

The Vikings loved to play all sorts of games. Many of these required clever tactics, which in real life were useful battlefield skills. Viking outdoor sports often attracted crowds at public festivals and assemblies. Sports helped train men for combat and seafaring, but could lead to injuries.

## Viking gamers

These walrus ivory chesspieces were found on the Isle of Lewis in Scotland. The Vikings also played a board game called hnefatafl, in which the king piece must be defended from attack.

Bishop piece with headdress and staff

## ! WOW!

The Vikings used skis for **travel** and **hunting**, not just for fun. In Norway, people have been skiing for over **7,000 years**.

# Outdoor sports

The Vikings loved outdoor sports. If a sports event turned into a violent brawl (fight), that was all part of the fun for a Viking.

King piece with crown

**Weightlifting and tug-of-war**
Storytellers loved to describe heroic feats of strength. Heavy boulders were used for weightlifting. Tug-of-war built up the strong muscles a Viking needed to row longships.

**Wrestling**
This sport could be done indoors or outdoors. Wrestlers grappled and tried to throw their opponents to the ground. This kind of activity was extremely dangerous.

**Ballgames**
Vikings played team games with a bat and ball, such as knattleikr. We don't know the rules, but it was an extreme contact sport. Games could last all day!

**Swimming**
From an early age, children would play and splash in the lakes and fjords. Swimming races and water games were popular with adults, too.

# Words and music

Being able to entertain people with poetry or music was an important Viking skill. The Vikings loved to hear exciting stories and poems about gods, goddesses, and heroes. They also liked riddles, and playing with words. Vikings described things in unusual ways, such as calling the sea "the ship's road".

## Making music

We don't know much about Viking music, as they did not write it down using notes. We know that Vikings danced, sang, and enjoyed festivals throughout the year. Travelling musicians would visit the halls of the jarls. Some Viking musical instruments have survived for us to study.

## Singing along

A stringed instrument called a lyre was popular among the Vikings. Lyres were frames made from wood, with strings that could be plucked. A musician could sing or speak along with the music.

A copy of a lyre from the 7th century.

**Playing a bone flute**

## Signalling horn

A horn without holes drilled in it had a limited range of notes but could be played very loudly. A blast on a horn could be heard above the noise of battle or on a hunting trip. It was used to sound the alarm or gather a group of people in one place.

## Skilful poets

From the 800s, poets called skálds performed in the halls of kings. They often sang the praises of their host, and if all went well they could be richly rewarded. Skálds liked to show off their clever use of language using different types of poetry.

## Horn blowers

Cattle or goat horns could be drilled with holes and played as musical instruments. They worked like modern wind instruments, such as recorders or flutes. Horns were often played at outdoor festivals, because they could be heard above the dancing and singing.

A skáld with a harp reciting a poem

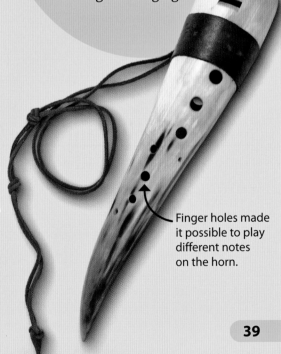

Finger holes made it possible to play different notes on the horn.

# Writing in runes

Vikings spoke a language called Old Norse. It could be written down using letters called runes. The rune alphabet or "futhark" is named after its first six letters (f-u-th-a-r-k). It varied over the ages and from one region to another.

## Jelling stone

This is a copy of a stone carved with runes, and with colour painted on. It was put up in Jelling, Denmark, by King Harald "Bluetooth", in about 965.

## Later writing

During the Viking age, poems and stories were spoken aloud so they could be passed on by word of mouth. Later writers heard the stories and wrote them down in books, using the modern alphabet.

*Galdrakver* book of Icelandic sagas, 1670

**The Sagas**
These are exciting stories about the kings of Norway, families in Iceland, and ancient legends. Some of them are historical accounts.

## Carving runes

Runes were made up of straight lines, designed for carving onto stone, wood, or bone. They were often used to label wooden objects with people's names.

Chiselling runes

### Family memories

Harald Bluetooth had the Jelling stone made in memory of his parents after they died. The writing says: "King Harald ordered this monument made in memory of Gormr, his father, and in memory of Thyrvé, his mother". Harald describes himself as the man "who won for himself all of Denmark and Norway and made the Danes Christian."

### The Eddas

These include a guide to the verse of the skálds (the poets of the Viking world), and were the first written versions of ancient tales about gods and heroes.

The oldest surviving handwritten text from the *Poetic Edda*.

### Snorri Sturluson

Snorri (1179–1241) was an Icelandic writer who lived after the Viking age. He wrote the *Prose Edda*, which told Viking stories.

# Art styles

The Vikings showed off their artistic skills through metalwork and jewellery, and with objects made from carved stone, walrus ivory, and wood. They loved detailed, swirling patterns, and designs of animals and monsters. The Vikings decorated their weapons, ships, cradles, wagons, and treasure chests. The style of art varied over the years, and from one region to another.

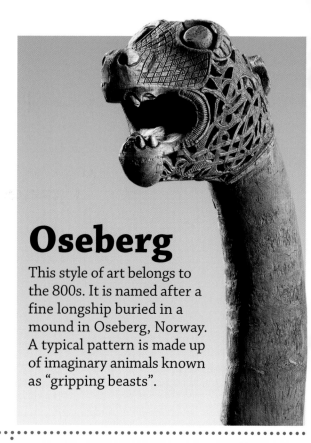

## Oseberg

This style of art belongs to the 800s. It is named after a fine longship buried in a mound in Oseberg, Norway. A typical pattern is made up of imaginary animals known as "gripping beasts".

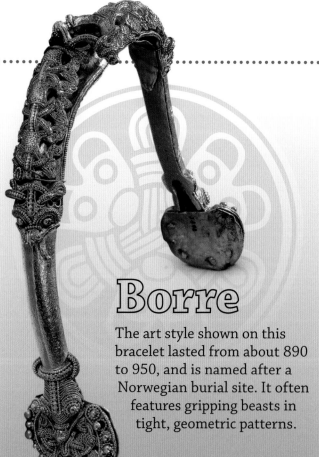

## Borre

The art style shown on this bracelet lasted from about 890 to 950, and is named after a Norwegian burial site. It often features gripping beasts in tight, geometric patterns.

## JELLING

The animal outlines on this silver cup are in the Jelling style, which is named after a royal burial site in Denmark. The cup may have belonged to King Gormr the Old, Harald Bluetooth's father.

# MAMMEN

This ceremonial iron axehead from Mammen, in Denmark, is decorated with silver wire. It dates from about 970 and its interlinked patterns show a bird – if you can untangle the design!

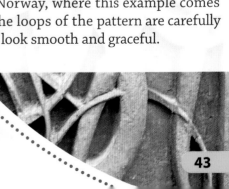

## Ringerike

Norway's Ringerike region gave its name to a style of gravestone carving. This stone slab, shown with restored colour, dates from about 1030. It was found in London, England, and may have belonged to Viking settlers.

## Urnes or Runestone

The final style of Viking animal art lasted into the 1100s. It is named after the wooden church of Urnes in Norway, where this example comes from. The loops of the pattern are carefully cut to look smooth and graceful.

# Dress like a Viking

Vikings wore simple, practical clothes made of wool and linen. They liked bright colours and jewellery. They wore cloaks of wool or fur, and covered their shoulders with woollen shawls to stay warm.

## Women's clothing
Women wore a woollen pinafore dress over a long shift, called a serk. Shoulder straps were fastened by brooches.

**Spindle**
Drop spindles were used to twist wool fibres into yarn for weaving.

**Pleats**
Pleated linen sleeves were the height of fashion for women's serks in the 900s.

**Layers**
Undergarments could be made of linen or wool.

## Trading silk

Luxury fabrics, such as shimmering silks, were brought back by merchants from the markets of Western Asia and Constantinople.

## Men's clothing

Men wore a woollen over-tunic called a kyrtill. Trousers were usually a straight shape.

**Beard**
Men kept their hair clean and the beard neatly trimmed.

**Tunic**
The necks and cuffs of the tunic were often decorated with braid. Clothing was used to show how important people were.

**Belt**
Both men and women hung useful things from their belts, such as knives, pouches, and keys.

**Leather boots**
Vikings wore boots, shoes, and slippers made from leather or goatskin.

## Jewellery

Jewellery could be made from cheap metal such as bronze, or from animal horn. More expensive jewellery was made from silver or gold. Precious jewellery was a way of showing and storing wealth.

**Brooches**
Two large brooches fastened the straps on women's dresses. Smaller ones fastened shawls.

**Cloak pins**
Long metal pins and ring-brooches were used for fastening heavy cloaks.

**Beads**
Beads made of glass or precious stones were worn hung between brooches, or as part of necklaces.

### ODIN
*King of the gods*

Odin is a one-eyed sky god, and king of all the gods. He lives in a great hall called Valhalla. He is the lord of victory, wisdom, runes (writing), healing, and death. He carries a magical spear called Gungnir.

### FREYJA
*Goddess of children and growth*

Freyja is a goddess of beauty, children, and love. She is the Lady of Fólkvangr, a heavenly field, which welcomes half of those who die in battle. The other half go to Valhalla.

# Gods and goddesses

The Vikings believed that a huge tree called Yggdrasil was the centre of the universe. In its branches were nine worlds filled with different beings. The powerful Viking gods lived in a world called Asgard, while humans lived in Midgard. In the 11th century, Vikings began to believe in Christianity.

## LOKI
### *The trickster*

Loki is a trickster and a thief. He is sometimes wicked and sometimes helpful. He is able to change shape, and can appear as an animal or as a woman.

## THOR
### *God of thunder*

The Vikings knew that when thunder and lightning raged, red-headed Thor was fighting a giant with his great hammer. Thor is the son of Odin. He rides a chariot pulled by goats.

## FRIGG
### *Goddess of childbirth and wisdom*

Frigg is the wife of Odin and the mother of Baldr, god of light. She can see into the future. She lives in Fensalir, a splendid hall built in the marshes.

**WOW!**

**Asgard** and **Midgard** were linked by a **rainbow bridge** called the Bifrost.

# A Norse tale

The Vikings loved to tell stories about their gods and goddesses. The gods were powerful, but they also made mistakes, just like humans. In this story, the trickster Loki almost gets into a fight with Thor.

Thor was the god of storms. He lived in Asgard with his wife, Sif. She was an earth goddess who protected families, and crops in the fields.

Sif was beautiful, and especially proud of her long hair. It was the colour of ripened corn.

One day, Loki was walking in the woods when he came across Sif, who was sleeping in the warm sun. Loki was a mischief-maker. As a prank, he cut off all her golden hair and ran away.

When Sif woke up and realised her hair was gone, she was horrified. She knew Thor would be mad with rage when he found out. Loki suddenly wondered if he'd gone too far.

Thor knew at once that Loki had been up to his usual tricks. Thunder roared and lightning crackled. The whole earth shook.

Thor found Loki and made him promise to replace the hair. Loki went into the darkness, to the magical forges and workshops of the dwarves called the Sons of Ivaldi.

The dwarves spun new, golden hair for Sif, and it shimmered in the summer sun. They also went on to make Mjöllnir, Thor's mighty war hammer. The Vikings called gold "Sif's hair".

## Grave goods

Family members put a dead person's most precious objects in their grave to show off their status. For example, a blacksmith might be buried with all his tools.

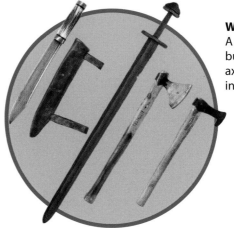

**Weapons**
A warrior might be buried with his sword, axe, or shield for use in the afterlife.

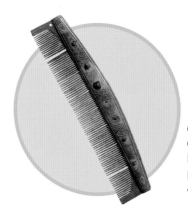

**Comb**
Combs carved from antler, bone, or walrus ivory were prized possessions for men and women of all classes.

**Spindle and wool**
Tools for spinning and weaving have been found, as well as textiles and embroidery.

**FACT FILE**

» **Name:** Ale's Stones

» **Location:** Skåne

» **Country:** Sweden

» **Info:** Some ancient burial sites were marked with stones in the shape of a ship.

# Afterlife

Life was hard in medieval times and many Vikings died young. Half of the warriors who died in battle were believed to feast forever with Odin in his great hall, called Valhalla. Freyja was said to welcome the other half to her hall, as well as women.

**Utensils**
Spoons, dishes, cooking pots, and pans might all prove useful in the next world.

**Jewellery**
The most precious grave goods included brooches, pendants, necklaces, and rings.

**Clothing**
Fragments of Viking clothes have survived in some graves, which helps us learn about what they wore.

# Meet the expert

Boatbuilder Søren Nielsen is the Head of Maritime Craft at the Viking Ship Museum in Roskilde, Denmark. He tells us about building the *Sea Stallion*, a reconstructed longship.

**Q: How did you become a boatbuilder?**

**A:** As a child, I loved to sail. As an adult, I was trained for four years as an apprentice wooden boatbuilder. I learned how to choose the right tree in the forest for the right job in the boat, and how to cut beautiful lines in the wood. There is always something new to learn and that makes it fun to continue.

**Q: How did you know what a Viking longship should look like?**

**A:** In 1956, a couple of fishermen caught some ship parts in their net when they were fishing in the Roskilde Fjord. Archaeologists investigated the ships and found them to be over 1,000 years old. The ships, including the one that we based our ship the *Sea Stallion* on, were made of thousands of parts. These

The *Sea Stallion* on its trial voyage from Roskilde to Dublin, Ireland.

**Rough seas**
The *Sea Stallion* braves the choppy waters of the English channel near Dover, 2008.

parts were collected and exhibited at the Viking Ship Museum, where they can be seen today.

**Q: You decided to construct a Viking longship based on these discoveries. Tell us about the design of the *Sea Stallion*.**

**A:** Viking longships were built using oak or pine planks. The planks overlapped with each other (clinker building) and were fastened with iron rivets. The planks create a hull (the main body of the ship), which is held together by ribs made of oak on the inside. The ribs are like the ship's skeleton. My job during the construction of the *Sea Stallion* was to look at the details of the original ship. I had to make sure we built a ship the same shape as the original by keeping a lot of measurements. It was also my job to organize the work and employ the people needed to solve the task, and to make sure that we did not spend more money than we had for the project.

**Q: Who else did you work with on the ship-building project?**

I worked with experts such as archaeologists and wood specialists. As a craftsman, there are a lot of things about the Viking age I do

The *Sea Stallion* takes shape, 2004. It can carry at least 60 people.

not know about, which the archaeologist does – just as an archaeologist cannot build a boat! By co-operating, we can illuminate different parts of the Viking Age.

**Q: What special equipment did you use?**

**A:** The *Sea Stallion* was built using different axes, knives, planing tools and drills – no saws. Our goal was to build the ship with the same tools and materials, and in the same shape as the old Viking ship. If we had made it stronger or weaker, we would not learn about how the Vikings sailed their ships 1,000 years ago.

**Q: What is it like to sail in the longship?**

**A:** I wrote this in my diary during a voyage from Dublin to Denmark on the *Sea Stallion*: "Over half of the crew is seasick. We take a lot of sea spray across the side, especially in the foreship right in front. The crew in the front has got a lot of water down their neck. The ship is doing great, even though it bumps and twists in the sea. The ship, as we have reconstructed it, stays strong, but it would be very worn by a sea voyage."

Søren planing the boat's stern

# After the Vikings

When the Vikings set out on journeys from their homelands in different parts of Scandinavia, they changed history. In some cases, the places they attacked became their new homes as they mixed with the local people. The influence of Viking culture can still be seen in many places.

Sculpture of a Viking, Iceland

### Iceland
The Vikings settled in Iceland in the 9th century and modern Icelanders are the descendents of these Viking pioneers. The Icelandic parliament was started as a Viking Thing in 930, and Icelandic laws are still based on Viking ones.

**The Dublin Stein**
The carved face is of Ivar the Boneless.

### Dublin
This stone pillar in modern Dublin is a copy of one that was put up in the Viking Age. It showed sailors where to tie up their longships.

### Scandinavian countries
The Viking homelands became strong Scandinavian kingdoms. The language and culture of modern Norway, Sweden, and Denmark all come from the Vikings.

Flag of Norway

Flag of Sweden

Flag of Denmark

Up Helly Aa festival,
Shetland

People from Lerwick dressed up as a jarl (Viking chieftain) and his men.

## The Normans

The Vikings won a large area of northern France in 911. They settled down and married with the Franks who lived there. The local people called the Vikings the "Northmen", and eventually they became known as the Normans.

## Up Helly Aa

This festival is held each winter in the town of Lerwick, Shetland. It is inspired by the Viking period of Scottish history and includes the burning of a wooden longship.

**Bayeux tapestry**
William the Conqueror invading England in 1066.

**Borgund stave church**
One of Norway's most beautiful medieval stave churches.

## Stave church

When the Vikings became Christians, they came up with their own church designs. This timber, or 'stave' church was built about 800 years ago in Borgund, Norway. It used all the woodworking skills of the old Vikings.

To play, take turns rolling a die.

## START

### Find a new home

You are the leader of a Viking clan. The homelands are getting overcrowded and you need to find a new place to live. Overcome the obstacles to create a settlement!

**1** **Loading the ship takes a long time. Miss a turn!**
For a sea voyage you must take all your food and clothes with you.

**2**

**14**

**13** **Land ahoy! Send scouts to check it's safe and wait until they return. Miss a turn.**
A scout goes on ahead and reports back to the main group.

**12**

**11** **Seagulls appear, which means land is nearby. Move forward 3 spaces!**
Seabirds such as gulls live on coasts, so if you spot one, you know land is near.

Seagull

**15** **You've landed! Move ahead 1 space to explore.**
The Vikings were brave settlers and often had to explore exciting new places.

**16**

**17**

**18** **It is getting dark and a storm is brewing. Move back 2 spaces.**
Settlers had to be tough to face the difficulties of creating a new home.

# A Viking adventure

When the Viking homelands became overcrowded, a group of people would pack their things and travel over the sea to find a new place to live. Being a settler was a hard life, and there were many challenges that had to be overcome in order to start a new settlement.

Brown bear

**27**

**28** **A stranger appears and offers to take you to his village. Go straight to the finish!**
The Vikings were good at mixing with local people when they wanted to.

**3** The winds begin to blow – you are ready to launch. Move ahead 3 spaces.
A longship could be moved by rowing but good winds helped it go fast.

**4**

**5** Rough waters ahead. Move back 1 space.
The Vikings were expert sailors. They looked at the waves to predict where the sea would take them.

**6**

**10**

**9** The crew is hungry and tired from rowing. Rest to eat and regain strength. Miss a turn.
When travelling, the Vikings ate whatever local food they could find or steal.

**8**

Fresh fish

**7** Read the currents to show which direction you should go in.
The Vikings were good at directions. They looked at the sun, sky, currents, and clouds to find their way.

**19**

**20** Lightning flashes. It is Thor! The lightning reveals a safe place in the woods. Move ahead 3 spaces.
The Vikings often asked the god of thunder for help and protection.

**21**

Thor's hammer

**22** You set up camp. It is time to rest. Miss a turn.
New settlers had to build their own houses in order to have a warm, safe place to live.

**26** A huge bear blocks your path. Go back 3 spaces.
The Vikings hunted bears for their fur but they could be dangerous animals to come across.

**25**

Manx Loaghtan sheep

**24** You hear goats and sheep somewhere in the distance. You must be near a farm. Move forward 1 space.
Goats and sheep could be eaten or milked.

**23**

**29**

**30** This land has a cold climate. It will be tough to settle here. Go back 1 space.
It was hard to grow food in icy places such as Greenland.

# You founded a settlement!
You have overcome the dangers and found a place to build your new settlement. Hopefully it will be a success and more Vikings will come and join you here.

**FINISH**

# Viking facts and figures

The Vikings were warriors and raiders, but they were also great makers and builders. Here are some amazing Viking facts.

The Vikings gave their swords names, such as Killer or Leg-biter.

**My name is Adder**

**My name is Fierce**

The longest longhouse ever found is almost as long as **Big Ben is tall** (83 m to 96 m or 272 ft to 315 ft).

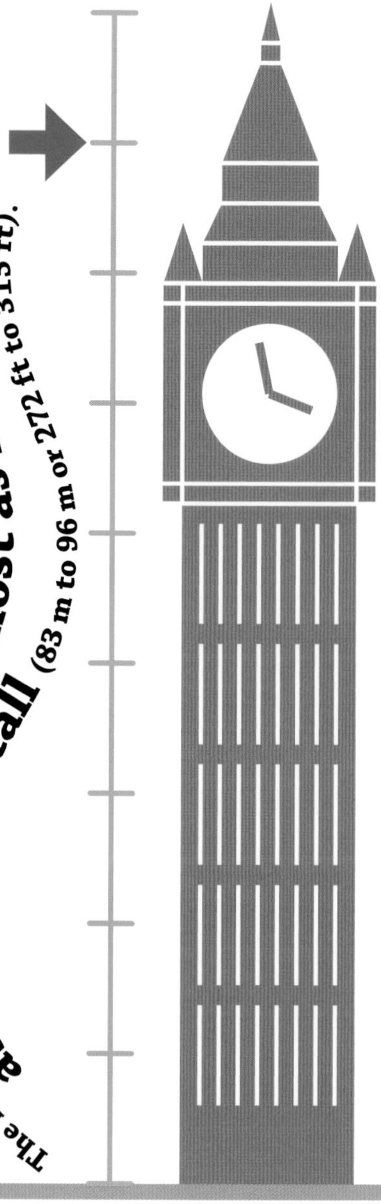

## 15

horses were buried in the Oseberg ship. It also contained 6 dogs, 2 cows, 5 beds, and 3 sleighs.

## 14,295

silver coins were part of the largest Viking treasure hoard ever found.

**Lindholm Høje**

# With more than 700 graves,

the Viking cemetery in Lindholm Høje, Denmark is one of the largest in the world.

**The Vikings used whale and seal skin to make strong ships' ropes.**

**Vikings made waterproof clothes out of animal skins rubbed with beeswax.**

# 30

Vikings were needed to sail an average longship.

# 300 ships and 9,000

men sailed with Harald when he invaded England in 1066.

# Glossary

Here are some words that are useful for you to know when learning all about the Vikings.

**Asgard** Mythical world of the Viking gods

**Althing** Icelandic parliament

**blacksmith** Skilled worker who heats and hammers metal to make tools and weapons

**byre** Shed for animals

**byrnie** Mail shirt

**boss** Raised, round piece in the centre of a shield

**Edda** Collection of books in which Viking tales were written down by writers living after the Viking Age

**fjord** Strip of sea that goes inland, especially in Scandinavia

**Folkvángr** Mythical field where the goddess Freyja took dead Vikings

**fort** Strong buildings that Viking kings could use to protect themselves, or show their power

**Freyr** Viking god of fertility

**Freyja** Goddess of love and beauty

**Frigg** Goddess of motherhood and wife of Odin

**hnefatafl** Viking board game, where the aim was to protect the king

**hoard** Collection of valuable treasure

**homeland** An area or region from which people originally come, Scandinavia for the Vikings

**Hugin** One of Odin's magical ravens

**hull** Main body of a boat or ship

**jarl** Noble or chief

**karl** Ordinary, free person in Viking society

**knarr** Viking cargo ship

**kyrtill** Tunic worn by Viking men

A **blacksmith** hammers metal.

**Loki** God of trickery and cunning

**longship** Long, narrow ship designed for speed, which the Vikings used for their raids

**loom** A wooden frame on which cloth can be woven

**lyre** Musical instrument with a wooden frame and strings

**mail** Armour made from metal rings linked together

**Midgard** Mythical world where humans lived

**Miklagard** Viking name for Constantinople (now Istanbul)

**Mjölnir** Magical hammer made for Thor by dwarfs

**Munin** One of Odin's ravens

**Normans** People of Northern France, descended from Vikings

**Odin** King of the gods and husband of the goddess Frigg

**Old Norse** Language of the Vikings

**raid** Sudden attack

**runes** Viking letters made up of straight lines

**sagas** Viking tales of gods, heroes, monsters, and adventures

**Scandinavia** Area of Northern Europe covering Norway, Sweden, and Denmark.

**serk** Shift or loose shirt

**Sif** Long-haired Viking Earth goddess

**skáld** Court entertainer who told poems about heroes and battles to please the king or another person

**Sleipnir** Odin's eight-legged horse

**Thing** Assembly of Vikings, where free men discussed issues in their local area

**Thor** God of thunder and lightning

**thralls** Slaves

**Valhalla** Odin's hall in the afterlife, where dead warriors were taken

**valkyrie** Mythical woman who carried dead warriors to the afterlife

A face guard protected a warrior's eyes and nose.

**warp** Threads that go up and down on a loom

**wattle-and-daub** Building material made from sticks and mud or clay

**weft** Threads that are woven from side to side on a loom

**Yggdrasil** Mythical tree connecting the nine worlds of Norse mythology, including Asgard and Midgard

A drilled horn could be used to play a tune.

# Index

# Acknowledgements

**The publisher would like to thank the following people for their assistance:** Polly Goodman for proofreading, Helen Peters for compiling the index, Richard Leeney for photography, Dan Crisp for illustrations, Mohd Zishan for illustrations, Romi Chakraborty for design and technical supervision, and Harish Aggarwal for helping with cutouts. The publishers would also like to thank the Viking re-enactors from Vikings of Middle England (www.vikingsof.me). Vilia Kane (Cei), Jason Green (Yngvar), Emma-Jane Anderson (Katla), Alastair Anderson (Angus), Chloe Cronogue (Throst), Alan Ball (Kael), Ezra Cronogue-Ball, Brinley Stringfellow (Brin), Harry Andrews (Ranulf), and also Riley Hobson for modelling.

The publisher would like to thank the following for their kind permission to reproduce their photographs:

(Key: a-above; b-below/bottom; c-centre; f-far; l-left; r-right; t-top)

2 **Statens Historiska Museum:** (bl) 3 **Dorling Kindersley:** Gary Ombler / Vikings of Middle England (crb). **Dreamstime.com:** Lucian Milasan / Miluxian (br); Odua (bl) 4 **Alamy Stock Photo:** World History Archive (bl) 7 **Dreamstime.com:** Jorisvo (bc); Amanda Lewis (br) **10-11 Getty Images:** National Geographic 11 **Kulturhistorisk Museum, Universitetet i Oslo:** Ove Holst (crb). **Nationalmuseet, Denmark:** (cr) 12 **Dorling Kindersley:** Gary Ombler / Vikings of Middle England (cl) 13 **Dorling Kindersley:** Gary Ombler / Vikings of Middle England (br/axe). **The Metropolitan Museum of Art, New York:** Rogers Fund, 1955 (br/sword) 14 **Lofotr Vikingmuseum, Borg in Lofoten, Norway:** UiO (tc). **Statens Historiska Museum:** (br) 15 **123RF.com:** Sergey Novikov (bc). **Kulturhistorisk Museum, Universitetet i Oslo:** UiO (crb). **Nationalmuseet, Denmark:** (tl) 17 **Kulturhistorisk Museum, Universitetet i Oslo:** University of Oslo / Ove Holst (bc). **Museum Victoria, Melbourne:** (cl). **Statens Historiska Museum:** (tc, tr, cr) 18 **Statens Historiska Museum:** (crb) 19 **Alamy Stock Photo:** ART Collection (clb); Cindy Hopkins (tl). **Dreamstime.com:** Lucian Milasan / Miluxian (tr) 20 **Alamy Stock Photo:** Antony McAulay (bl) **20-21 Nationalmuseet, Denmark:** Niels Elswing 24 **Lofotr Vikingmuseum, Borg in Lofoten, Norway:** Kjell Ove Storvik (bc). **Statens Historiska Museum:** (tr) 25 **123RF.com:** Leonid Spektor (tr). **Alamy Stock Photo:** Cindy Hopkins (tl) 30 **Alamy Stock Photo:** Ashley Cooper (c). **Dreamstime.com:** Tiina Tuomaala (br) **30-31 Dreamstime.com:** Daria Rybakova / Podarenka (c) 31 **123RF.com:** Steve Byland (tl). **Dreamstime.com:** Isselee (cl). **Lofotr Vikingmuseum, Borg in Lofoten, Norway:** Kjell Ove Storvik (bc) 32 **123RF.com:** Nikolai Grigoriev (br) 33 **Statens Historiska Museum:** (tl) 34

**Statens Historiska Museum:** (tr) 35 **Statens Historiska Museum:** (tl, tc) **36-37 Lofotr Vikingmuseum, Borg in Lofoten, Norway:** UiO (c) 36 **The Metropolitan Museum of Art, New York:** Gift of J. Pierpont Morgan, 1917 (cr) 38 **Alamy Stock Photo:** Granger Historical Picture Archive (br) 39 **Alamy Stock Photo:** INTERFOTO (bl) 40 **Getty Images:** Universal History Archive (bc) 41 **Alamy Stock Photo:** Ivy Close Images (bl); MediaWorldImages (cra); Rolf Richardson (bc) 42 **Kulturhistorisk Museum, Universitetet i Oslo:** UiO / Kirsten J. Helgeland (tr); University of Oslo / Eirik Irgens Johnsen (bl). **Statens Historiska Museum:** (br) 43 **Alamy Stock Photo:** John Warburton-Lee Photography (tr). **Nationalmuseet, Denmark:** Roberto Fortuna and Kira Ursem (cla). **Statens Historiska Museum:** (bl) 45 **Statens Historiska Museum:** (cra, cr, crb, br) **46-47 Dreamstime.com:** Pavalache Stelian (background) 50 **Dorling Kindersley:** Dave King / The Science Museum, London (cra); Gary Ombler / Vikings of Middle England (tc, tc/axes); Gary Ombler / The Combined Military Services Museum (CMSM) (tc/sword). **Statens Historiska Museum:** (cla) **50-51 Alamy Stock Photo:** Sunshine Pics (b) 51 **Dorling Kindersley:** Gary Ombler / Vikings of Middle England (tr) 52 **The Viking Ship Museum, Denmark:** Werner Karrasch (tr, bl) 53 **The Viking Ship Museum, Denmark:** Werner Karrasch (tr, bl) 54 **Alamy Stock Photo:** deadlyphoto.com (cr); Joan Gil (cl) 55 **Alamy Stock Photo:** Aurelian Images (cr); Dave Donaldson (tl) 56 **123RF.com:** Aleksandar Mijatovic (c). **Dorling Kindersley:** Stephen Oliver (tc). **Lofotr Vikingmuseum, Borg in Lofoten, Norway:** Kjell Ove Storvik (tr) 57 **Alamy Stock Photo:** Ashley Cooper (cb). **Statens Historiska Museum:** (c) 58 **Dorling Kindersley:** Peter Anderson / Universitets Oldsaksamling, Oslo (bl); Gary Ombler / Vikings of Middle England (cl). **The Metropolitan Museum of Art, New York:** Rogers Fund, 1955 (cr/sword) 59 **Alamy Stock Photo:** Iconotec (tl) 61 **Dorling Kindersley:** Gary Ombler / Vikings of Middle England (tr) 62 **Alamy Stock Photo:** Ashley Cooper (tl) 64 **Dreamstime. com:** Lucian Milasan / Miluxian (tl)

**Cover images:** *Front:* Alamy Stock Photo: Granger Historical Picture Archive cra / (lyre), INTERFOTO cb, Rocky Reston ca/ (horn); **Dorling Kindersley:** Gary Ombler / Vikings of Middle England ca/ (helmet); **Museum Victoria, Melbourne:** tr; **Statens Historiska Museum:** cra; *Back:* Lofotr Vikingmuseum, Borg in Lofoten, Norway: UiO cl; **Statens Historiska Museum:** tr; *Front Flap:* Alamy Stock Photo: Ashley Cooper ca, Sabena Jane Blackbird c; **Dorling Kindersley:** Gary Ombler / Vikings of Middle England c/ (axe); **The Metropolitan Museum of Art, New York:** Rogers Fund, 1955 cl/ (1); **Statens Historiska Museum:** clb, bl; *Back Flap:* **Dorling Kindersley:** Gary Ombler / The University of Aberdeen c, Gary Ombler / Wardrobe Museum crb.w **Endpaper images:** *Front:* Alamy Stock Photo: ART Collection (Battle of, Stamford Bridge), Classic Image (William the Conqueror), GM Photo Images (Erik the Red); **Depositphotos Inc:** MennoSchaefer (Lindisfarne); **Statens Historiska Museum:** (pendant);

All other images © Dorling Kindersley
For further information see:
www.dkimages.com

## About the consultant

Dr Ragnhild Ljosland is an expert in the history of the Viking age. She has a PhD in Sociolinguistics from the Norwegian University of Science and Technology in 2008. She has worked at the University of the Highlands and Islands Institute for Northern Studies since 2009.

My Findout facts:

PILLGWENLLY   28-09-18

# Long branch runes

The 16 letter runic alphabet is called the "futhark" after its first six letters. The "long branch" runes shown here were most popular in Denmark. In Sweden, a similar alphabet called the "short twig" was used.

f   u   th

a   r   k   h   n

i   a   s   t   b

m   l   z